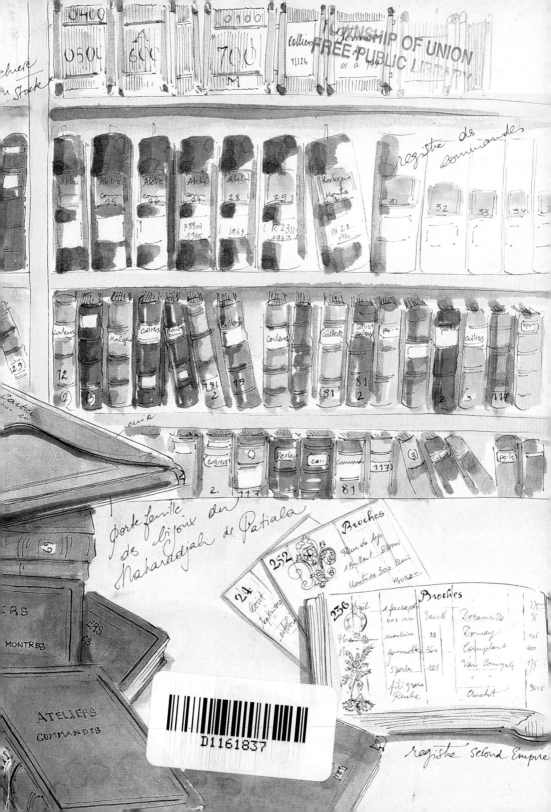

Cartier

First published in the United States of America in 1997
by UNIVERSE PUBLISHING
A Division of Rizzoli International Publications, Inc.
300 Park Avenue South
New York, NY 10010

and THE VENDOME PRESS

Front cover photograph: Carved coral chimera mystery clock, 1930.
Collection R. Esmerian Inc., New York

ISBN 0-7893-0087-7

Printed and bound it Italy

Library of Congress Catalog Card Number: 97-060142

UNIVERSE OF DESIGN

Cartier

BY PHILIPPE TRÉTIACK

UNIVERSE / VENDOME

With the foundation of Cartier's the jewellers in 1847 began one of the most glorious chapters in the history of the decorative arts. The century and a half that has elapsed since then has yielded many masterpieces – necklaces, bracelets, pearls and jewelry of all kinds – that epitomize their age while retaining a timeless quality.

Louis-François Cartier (1819–1904) was the son of a manufacturer of powder-horns. At the age of twenty-eight, he took over the Paris workshop of his employer Picard in the Rue Montorgueil before setting up business in 1853 at 9 Rue Neuve-des-Petits-Champs, between the Bourse and the Palais-Royal, and selling only to private customers. How could he possibly have guessed the fame that he would later enjoy, that it would be his destiny to capture the latent fire of gemstones which would blaze and sparkle on the foreheads of kings and the hands of queens? The fact is that Cartier was blessed with an extraordinary gift. This first became evident in 1859, when he opened his new showrooms on the Boulevard des Italiens. There, at the vibrant heart of Paris, began his association with the great couturier Charles Frédéric Worth. An eccentric, who at that time always dressed in the style of Rembrandt (like the composer Richard Wagner), Worth was about to launch the fashion for the crinoline and at a stroke, in the reverberations that ensued, invent *haute couture*. This first collaboration between fabrics and precious stones marked the beginning of the close association that has existed ever since between fashion and the jeweller's art. Cartier, in making his jewelry the ultimate accompaniment of the fashionable outfits of the great and the good, became the craftsman, and subsequently artist, whose skills were indispensable to the reputation of the elegant woman. Henceforward the cream of European society would flock to his door. This marriage of minds was cemented two generations later by the marriage of Andrée Worth, the couturier's granddaughter, to Louis-Joseph, grandson of Louis-François Cartier.

Jeweller of kings, king of jewellers

In the meantime, in the cramped premises in the Rue Neuve-des-Petits-Champs, the house of Cartier was on the point of achieving its first great coup. Louis-François Cartier was aged thirty-six when the Countess of Nieuwerkerke first entered his shop in 1855. Over the next three years, she would acquire from him some fifty-five items. Her husband was the Superintendent of Fine Art to Napoleon III and also a friend of Princess Mathilde, niece of the great Napoleon I. The princess too gave Cartier commissions: Medusa-head cameos, earrings etc. And eventually the Empress Eugénie herself, wife of Napoleon III, ordered a silver tea-service. Cartier's prospects were transformed. Now in great demand, he moved to premises on the Boulevard des Italiens, just a stone's throw from the Palais Garnier, whose Napoleon-III style would later be regarded as epitomizing the age. Courts everywhere despatched ambassadors to investigate the jeweller everyone was praising to the skies, and in due course Cartier's became jeweller by special appointment to a number of royal households. Fifteen such warrants were granted between 1904 and 1939, appointing Cartier's an 'official purveyor' to the crowned heads of Europe. Among these were the royal warrants issued by King Edward VII of England (on the occasion of his marriage, Cartier's had to supply twenty-seven tiaras) and by Alfonso XIII of Spain in 1904, and in the following year by Carlos I of Portugal, by Tsar Nicholas II in 1907 and King Paramindr Maha Chulalongkorn of Siam in 1908 (the latter chose bracelets not singly but by the trayful!), by King George I of Greece in 1909, and eventually by King Zog of Albania in 1939. So numerous were they that Edward VII, while still Prince of Wales, described Louis Cartier as being the 'jeweller of kings as well as the king of jewellers'.

The bold originality of genius

the founder of Cartier's was endowed not only with a good head for business, but with an even stronger feeling for precious stones. Where gems were concerned, he was a genius. The other great names in jewelry – Eugène Fontenay, Charles Christofle and Fortunato Pio Castellani – were all influenced by the exhibition of the Campana Collection at the Louvre in 1861, consisting of ancient works of art recently acquired by Napoleon III. But Cartier combined Etruscan, Greek and Roman models with more contemporary designs. His sources of inspiration included the sculptor Jean-Baptiste Carpeaux's *La Danse* as well as animal motifs (horses, butterflies, crabs). People were astounded by his choice of subjects. Cartier's strength lay in remaining, like the rest of his colleagues, within the conventions of the day, while at the same time experimenting with a variety of stylistic influences. All of which was accomplished with an incredible purity of line. This represented the bold originality of genius. In the early years of the Third Republic, the increased tempo of life already anticipated the Belle Époque. Liberal France was experiencing an unprecedented growth in the decorative arts, reinvigorated by a series of technical innovations. After years of political wariness and suspicion towards France, with its reputation for revolts and revolutions, foreign clients finally plucked up courage to find their way again to the 'capital of the nineteenth century', to use the phrase coined by the German writer Walter Benjamin to describe the Paris of his time, the so-called City of Light. For everyone who was anyone in Europe, a visit to Cartier's establishment was a must.

For many celebrities it became part of the social round. It was almost as though the capital had acquired an extra *quartier*, the busiest of them all. In those days of economic growth, the clientèle was constantly expanding. The recent discovery of major diamond deposits in South Africa had resulted in prices falling sharply, thus bringing the luxury of owning fine jewelry within the reach of any member of the newly prosperous bourgeoisie.

Rue de la Paix

In 1874, Alfred Cartier (1841–1925) took over from his father the running of the shop in the Boulevard des Italiens, and in 1898 he was joined by his son Louis-Joseph (1875–1942). It was the latter who inherited his grandfather Louis-François's business acumen, and who would usher the firm into a new era. First he moved to premises in the Rue de La Paix, the epitome of luxury in Paris. In this, the most elegant street in the world, he rubbed shoulders with the perfume manufacturer Guerlain and the couturiers Frédéric Worth and Jacques Doucet. It was a time when everything was being questioned. Jewellers like Charles Lalique promoted the Art Nouveau style in which oriental influences were combined with European technical innovations. The poster artist Alphonse Mucha, the architect Hector Guimard and the glassmaker Émile Gallé are among its best-known exponents. However, Louis Cartier did not share the general enthusiasm for the style that had swept through Europe and was flourishing in Vienna, Brussels and Paris under a variety of names: the Secession, De Stijl and *style nouille*. His reluctance to go along with his colleagues' wholesale espousal of Art Nouveau was to inform and shape the entire future direction of Cartier designs. Louis Cartier was more traditionally inclined. He pored enthusiastically over old anthologies of eighteenth-century French art. Far into the night, he studied ironwork, lace and painting. He broadened the scope of his researches to include even the curling, intertwined patterns of Islamic and oriental art. His aim was to achieve a simplicity and purity of line that would enhance the floral motif which, in Art Nouveau, was too stylized and too distorted for his taste. Above all he felt a passionate desire to show off the beauty of diamonds. That was his obsession. His business involved precious stones, and he sought to display them to maximum advantage. This central aim dictated the entire ethos of the Cartier style. Concerned to play down the importance of settings and mounts, Louis was constantly seeking new ways of setting stones so that they would always appear light and unencumbered. And from this harking back to French tradition was born the famous '*style Guirlande*' or garland style that constitutes the Cartier trademark.

The garland style

the decision taken by Louis to cease working in silver sparked a revolution. He found this metal too malleable, and particularly disliked the fact that it was subject to oxidization and blackening. By candlelight this tendency may not have been such a disadvantage, but it suddenly assumed immense importance as electric lighting took over. Determined to move with the times, Louis turned instead to the use of platinum, and proceeded to develop the garland style featuring full, flowing curves that look as though they were drawn with the aid of compasses – symmetrical compositions in which the voids are as important as the solid elements in the design. Yet another masterstroke: placing emphasis on empty space. Louis wanted his diamonds to display all their sparkle and brilliance, allowing nothing extraneous to mask them or dim their fire. He rang the changes, experimenting with different motifs, and gradually the bow, the tassel and lace motifs emerged as the distinctive elements of a style that offered a clear alternative to the prevailing Art Nouveau. Louis was to bring to his era a committed classicism that would soon attract a host of discriminating admirers. By the close of the century his steady output included masterpieces in the form of dog-collars and laurel crowns.

Paris, London, New York

With success came prosperity, and the firm decided to go out and meet its clientèle on their own ground. Family loyalty served the interests of the firm well as the three brothers – Louis, Jacques (Théodule) and Pierre (Camille) – more or less divided up the Western world between them. The trust that existed between them was the basis for the future management of the firm. Jacques (1884–1942) opened the London branch in 1902 and Pierre (1878–1942) moved to New York seven years later. At this time the family also wanted to establish an outlet in St Petersburg in the wake of the enormous success there of enamelled *objets d'art* made by Carl Fabergé, a German jeweller descended from a French Huguenot family. Celebrated for his intricate jewelled Easter eggs, Fabergé also created a fashion for objects both expensive and practical – small clocks, cigarette cases and elaborate accessories – that were lapped up by the wealthy Russian bourgeoisie. Louis Cartier in his turn began producing the table clocks and gem-studded sculptures that rapidly established his reputation. He even made two eggs in the Fabergé manner, and members of the Russian aristocracy eagerly opened the doors of their palaces to him. Even so, Louis Cartier was hesitant about opening a permanent branch in the Russia of the Tsars, and eventually he decided merely to appoint a representative based in St Petersburg. It was a wise decision, and in the light of the subsequent revolutionary turmoil appears prescient. The Cartiers travelled the world. Jacques went East and visited Bahrain to discover how the splendid local pearls were fished. Demand grew constantly, encouraged by the success of Art Deco, with its emphasis on verticality rather than curves. In 1900, women's fashions too had undergone a revolution. Younger women were more active and involved in sport and hence wanted simpler clothes. Paul Poiret left Jacques Doucet to join Worth, where for the first time he designed simple dresses for everyday activities. One particular innovation was the hobble skirt which unleashed the fury of the Vatican. Jewelry was influenced by the new mood. Younger women sporting the short hair style known as the 'urchin cut' emphasized the straight lines of their dresses with longer and longer pendants. Drop earrings 8 centimetres long were quite usual. Pearls were about to come into their own.

Two strings of pearls

the world yearns for luxury and beauty, but in the years preceding the outbreak of the First World War a wave of social puritanism swept across Europe. The ostentatious display of jewels was less and less appreciated when industrial strikes and political revolutions were just around the corner. It is also true that the period then drawing to a close had been characterized by conspicuous consumption. Europe had gone overboard for lavish parties at which people flaunted their fortunes on their backs, wearing outfits of breathtaking splendour. With the craze for tiaras that had swept the courts of Europe, one needed eyes in the back of one's head. Crowned heads bobbed in unison on the dance floor, and the fact that swarms of private detectives hovered nearby merely added to the fun. Popular serials featured accounts of daring jewel thefts perpetrated by Arsène Lupin, Ruggles and the like. The international gentry flocked to Cartier's doors. The tiara was the height of fashion, and only the First World War dealt it a death blow. On the eve of the first shots being fired, the Princesse Jacques de Broglie organized a Gemstone Ball, during which the sea of gently undulating jewelled tiaras was almost indistinguishable from the crystal chandeliers. There was the *kokoshnik* or Russian tiara in the form of a cock's-comb; the bandeau or ribbon-shaped tiara, whose centre is not accentuated as in the case of the *kokoshnik*; the meander tiara inspired by ancient Greek ornament and the river Maiandros in Phrygia; the sun tiara; the plant and floral tiara; the wheat-ear tiara; the tiara with pendent drops. It was an apotheosis. For the last time, diamonds cast their glow over the lavish gowns worn by the pre-war jet set.

Now they gave way to strings of pearls, an altogether more modest choice – or apparently so. For it was not long before pearl necklaces became a consuming passion. On occasion they would change hands for the price one would expect to pay for a painting by Rembrandt. Eventually the market in pearls was to take a tumble, because of the Wall Street crash in 1929 and as a result of the discovery of 'black gold' in the countries of the Middle East. Attracted by wages far higher than they could earn from fishing, many of the pearl-fishers now sought work in the oilfields – and this at just the time when Japan began to step up its own production of cultured pearls, inferior in quality to the best natural specimens. Black pearls from Tahiti would suddenly become all the rage. Symbolic of the era as a whole was the deal that enabled Cartier's to open up in the heart of New York: the banker Morton F. Plant offered to exchange his magnificent town house at 653 Fifth Avenue for two strings of finest-quality pearls valued at a million dollars. Pierre Cartier did not hesitate for a moment.

The Ballets Russes

Over the years Cartier's refined its style. Although resistant to Art Nouveau, the three brothers were generally responsive to outside ideas. In Paris, the revelation of Diaghilev's Ballets Russes was one of the influences that was to transform and energize Cartier's production. In 1909, the talented draughtsman Charles Jacqueau joined the firm. He served his apprenticeship by accompanying Louis Cartier to Russia, and was subsequently to modify the garland style with a number of oriental additions. Ever curious and observant, he would devote many hours to sketching the plants and animals in the zoological gardens at Vincennes.

For the moment this gifted draughtsman was still very much feeling his way. Until, that is, the day he went to the Théâtre du Châtelet to see a performance of *Schéhérazade* given by the Ballet Russe. The impact was so great that its repercussions can still be felt in the Cartier style today. Charles Jacqueau was entranced by the golds and blues, the juxtapositions of strong colours, the excitingly different stage sets. He threw himself into work, and the designs he produced while 'under the influence' brought a breath of fresh air to modern jewelry: amethysts, emeralds, sapphires, even Japanese and Chinese pendants, took over from the Marie Antoinette style with its pastel shades on which Cartier's fame had hitherto depended. It was another of those characteristically bold strokes which had helped the Cartier firm to prosper. The combination of blue and green, the so-called Peacock design, reflects Charles Jacqueau's boldness and imagination, his willing-ness to take risks. The new combinations of colours might appeal to the clientèle or it might equally well appal them. Happily, Cartier's clients were people who recognized talent, and Viscountess Astor, an important customer of the day, was among the first to purchase a Peacock bandeau. The effect Cartier's had on the world of jewelry at that time was com-parable to the cataclysmic upheaval the Fauves brought about in paint-ing. Louis Cartier was continually exploring new artistic directions and new technical methods. To make more flexible armatures, for example, he had the idea of using the humble hairnet as a source of inspiration.

A clientèle originally based on the royal households had already expanded to take in the wealthiest stratum of the bourgeoisie. Now they were joined by celebrities from the world of show business, and even by a few high-class courtesans. Cartier's made jewelry for Sarah Bernhardt and the beautiful Caroline Otéro, and they in their turn became ambas-sadresses for the Cartier style. In those years of colonial expansion, when the Maghreb, Siam and Cochin China were in effect the extended national frontiers of France, the garland style reflected certain oriental influences. The result was eclectic, featuring ideas borrowed not only from exotic and distant lands but also from the ancient civilizations, then the subject of archeological excavations which were yielding a constant stream of buried treasures. It was the Valley of the Kings in Egypt that inspired all those variations on themes such as pyramids and obelisks encrusted with mother-of-pearl hieroglyphs. So charmingly did they complement the allure of precious stones that in 1929 King Fuad appointed Cartier's as an official purveyor to the Egyptian court, an honour confirmed by his successor, King Farouk, who commissioned from the establishment in the Rue de la Paix a number of luxury items and gadgets such as yoyos and toothpicks made of gold.

The Indian Empire

Well placed at the hub of these interrelated influences was India, especially as Cartier's London clientèle had important interests there. The Indian Empire, as it was known from 1858 while under British rule, offered an inexhaustible array of wonders and surprises. The Cartier firm lost no time in sending representatives to establish contact with the fabulously rich maharajahs, who could not wait to see the contents of their treasure-chests transformed into fine jewels. Using the most precious examples of gemstones that Rajasthan could provide, Cartier's would produce a profusion of necklaces and jewels. These are creations reflecting a cunning marriage of Cartier's expertise with Hindu influences. It was not long before pieces of jewelry displaying Indo-Persian inspiration were echoed in the Art Deco style in general. Foremost among these legendary Indian rulers was the Maharajah of Kapurthala, a passionate collector of clocks and watches. In his household he had a full-time employee whose job it was to keep wound his 250 precision-made timepieces, many of which came from the workshops in the Rue de la Paix.

A living reality

n 1925, when the modified garland style had already anticipated Art Déco, Louis Cartier had another of his inspired ideas. At the World's Fair (the Exposition Internationale des Arts Décoratifs et Industriels Modernes that gave the Art Déco style its name) in Paris, where he was an exhibitor, Cartier decided to display his wares not at the Grand Palais but in the Pavillon d'Élégance, alongside the couturier Lanvin. He was convinced that jewelry and precious stones ought to be shown to the public as a 'living reality'. The mannequins were styled in accordance with drawings by Modigliani and Brancusi. The geometric abstraction of modernism – already expressed in Art Déco jewelry featuring iridescent mother-of-pearl – was much to the fore. Cartier showed 150 pieces, the fruits of three years of dedicated work, including long earrings, brooches and belt-buckles, as well as bracelets made in 1923 in which flower and fruit motifs seem to explode with vibrant life and colour. The greens, reds and silvers of these quite exceptional pieces were to find their ultimate expression in the 'Tutti frutti' collection. Once again, by flying in the face of tradition, the house of Cartier had stolen a march on the rest.

Cartier time

perating at the luxury end of the jewelry trade, it was inevitable that the firm should develop an interest in clockmaking. Back in 1904, Louis Cartier had produced a watch intended as a tribute to the courage of the Brazilian aviator Santos-Dumont. With its clean lines suggestive of speed, anticipating Paul Morand's *L'homme pressé*, the model was produced commercially in 1911. A few years later came the 'Tank' watch, its brutalist form directly inspired by the newly developed military machine that, unfortunately, seemed destined to have a promising future. In the Cartier workshops the ingenious Maurice Coüet made a great leap forward with the line of 'mystery clocks', based on systems developed by Jean-Eugène Robert-Houdin in the mid-nineteenth century. The hands of these clocks appear to float inside a tranparent face. The mechanism that regulates them has simply disappeared from view, and the hands are seen moving on their own, as if by magic. In reality, each hand is fixed into a toothed glass disc that is driven by a worm screw, while the movement is hidden in the base. The illusion thus created – the almost palpable sense of the passing of time – makes these table and desk mystery clocks objects of total fascination. The 'Comet' clock, the pillar or gravity clock, the 'Turtle' clock, the 'Chimaera' clock, clocks in the classical, Chinese and Byzantine styles . . . all exploit effects of gravity graphically translated by intricate systems of cogwheels. Some of these clocks would come to be seen not only as masterpieces of their maker but of the horological profession as a whole.

The 'signature' Panther

during the Depression following the stock market crash of 1929, Louis Cartier found a formidable ally in Jeanne Toussaint. A friend of Coco Chanel, this extraordinary woman – later nicknamed 'Panther' – was to have overall control of Cartier creations for a period of twenty years. Although she was never a designer herself, her influence and talent were such that the Princess Bibesco one day complimented her for having 'perfumed the diamonds'. In 1933, Jeanne Toussaint took charge of *haute joaillerie*. In the latter years of Art Deco, she made the panther a cult item, a sort of trademark. She was always trying to come up with new ideas, and under her control the firm's technical department developed a whole series of inventions designed to combine solidity of construction with ease of use: clasps, clips modelled on clothes pegs, brooches made in parts that could be fitted together. Cartier's was emerging into the age of the modern accessory. A new 'Department S' was created, devoted to the production of luxury gifts and practical items such as lighters, pocket watches and belts. Many novel lines were produced, anticipating the range 'Les Must de Cartier', introduced in 1973. This was a different world, an entirely new departure, an attempt to provide an altogether more contemporary range of luxury goods.

Meanwhile, during the Second World War Cartier's activities were severely curtailed in France under the Occupation. It was from Cartier's London headquarters that General de Gaulle broadcast to the French nation, while the workshops there were commissioned to make badges of rank and decorations. When the Liberation came, the world was a different place. The changed circumstances were encapsulated by the brooch, created by Jeanne Toussaint and Pierre Lemarchand, in the form of an open cage and a bird singing – a concept of newly restored freedom. The world of fashion was reeling under the shock of Christian Dior's New Look. By exalting femininity, Paris recovered its leading position in the world of fashion and luxury items. As well as Dior, the city's couturiers included Balenciaga and later Jacques Fath and Pierre Balmain, attracting a wealthy clientèle, among whom were some of the world's most beautiful women. When both Louis and Jacques Cartier were lost to the business in 1942, the running of the firm in the Rue de la Paix devolved upon Jeanne Toussaint and Pierre Lemarchand. Together – just as Charles Jacqueau had done before them – they found inspiration at the zoo in Vincennes. The Cartier bestiary was already richly furnished with panther and zebra skins and turtle shells, used either as the basis for designs or as backgrounds against which the firm's creations could be displayed. Now the collection was augmented by further borrowings from the world of flora and fauna and from Asian cultures. Dragons and chimaeras were used to embellish table clocks, brooches and pendants, while symbolic elements derived from Germanic and Far Eastern myths were introduced for the first time into the Cartier repertoire. In 1954, Jeanne Toussaint revived the Chimaera style which had been hugely popular in the 1920s, but now she tamed the monster and transformed it into a lovable domestic pet. It was immediately adopted by the Baroness d'Erlanger and by the Hon. Mrs Fellowes, both of them passionate devotees of the jeweller's art.

Legendary clients

Chief among these were the Duke and Duchess of Windsor. In 1948, the Duke commissioned a Panther brooch for his wife. This consisted of a panther of speckled gold lying on top of a cabochon emerald weighing 116.74 carats. This three-dimensional panther was a first for Cartier's. The following year, it was once again the Windsors who purchased a cabochon sapphire weighing 152.35 carats decorated with a seated panther encrusted with diamonds interspersed with sapphires. The Hon. Mrs Fellowes, who vied with the Duchess of Windsor for the title of the world's best-dressed woman, commissioned a Panther brooch for herself, executed in sapphires and diamonds. In 1957, Princess Nina Aga Khan was the recipient of the most prestigious of all the Panther jewels: a jabot-pin, a pendant brooch and a bracelet with two panther's heads. Barbara Hutton, reputed to be the wealthiest heiress of the day, countered with a tiger – declaring it was the only animal that possessed no fine feelings.

Among leading French dignitaries, Marshal Foch and Marshal Pétain went to Cartier's for their ceremonial batons, while other notables ordered ceremonial swords. The first member of the Académie Française to seek the jeweller's services as sword-maker was the Duc de Gramont, in 1931. His was the first of a long series of academicians' swords produced by Cartier's, among them the one made for Jean Cocteau. In 1955, the poet commissioned a sword based on his own wonderful designs on the theme of Orpheus. His style was to have a substantial influence on the firm's later production. To him we owe the evocative and oft-quoted description of Cartier as 'a cunning magician, who can capture scraps of moonlight against a gold thread of sunlight'. A great admirer of the jeweller's style, he was the recipient of a magnificent ring made for him by his friend Louis Cartier. It consisted of three bands of gold, each in a different and symbolic colour – grey for friendship, yellow for constancy and pink for love – an altogether original piece displaying a rare simplicity and perfection.

Cartier's and the arts

In 1983, Cartier's decided to establish its own retrospective collection. Paradoxical as it may seem, the firm based in the Rue de la Paix owned almost no examples of its own creations. Since its foundation, the curator of the Cartier Collection, Éric Nussbaum, has managed to amass some 1,500 pieces. It was a heroic task. Auctions and private sales have provided the basis of the collection – but in any family the jewels are always the last things to be sold. Nineteenth-century pieces are few in number, for in those days it was the custom to break up jewels and tiaras and remodel them in the latest prevailing fashion. Of the extravaganzas originally commissioned by royal households, only examples pertaining to monarchies that no longer exist (Russia, Serbia, etc.) have occasionally come onto the market and thus found their way into the collection. The rest, like those owned by members of the British royal family, remain inaccessible.

Today, thanks to the existence of this expanding archival collection, fabulous exhibitions are organized all over the world, under the aegis of Franco Cologni, Cartier's Vice-President. To celebrate the firm's 150th anniversary in 1997, the Metropolitan Museum of Art in New York and the British Museum in London are jointly mounting a major exhibition, sponsored by Cartier's, featuring specially selected items from the collection. It is to this extraordinary archive that Micheline Kanouï, in charge of Cartier's Création Joaillerie since 1980, has turned for inspiration. It provides the basis for combining innovation with fidelity to the spirit of the Cartier style. Every year, more than fifteen hundred examples of *de luxe* jewelry and timepieces, as well as special commissions, are designed, manufactured and executed by Cartier's in Paris. In addition, every four years, she produces a 'theme' collection of over a hundred items of jewelry. Topics have included the power of signs, varieties of gold and precious stones, the grandeur that was Egypt and the mysteries of India. In 1996, and to celebrate the forthcoming millennium, she chose pieces for her sixth Nouvelle Joaillerie collection as a celebration of the creation of the universe. As she delves into precedent, adapting past styles, her contemporary approach is evident in her ability to highlight specific detail, the one-off piece, the out-of-the-ordinary commission. Inspired by that ultimate expression of what the name Cartier represents – the clocks with their concealed mechanisms – she has designed equally magical pocket watches that are *tours de force*. In a similar spirit, Alain Dominique Perrin, President of the company, took the decision in 1984 to establish the Cartier foundation for contemporary art. In approaching the architect Jean Nouvel to design the building for it on the Boulevard Raspail in Paris, he demonstrated that past glories could most fittingly be celebrated in a modern architectural setting where, once again, the mechanisms are concealed: the very incarnation of the spirit of the house of Cartier.

Cartier
13 Rue de la Paix
Paris

Cartier Ltd.
175 New Bond Street, W.
London.

Cartier Inc.
Fifth Avenue and Fifty-second Street
New York.

Jacques Cartier lors de son voyage à Bahrein en 1911.

Dubar de Delhi 1911.

Crown gewels
designed and Mounted
for
H.H. The Maharaja Dhiraj
of Patiala
by
Cartier

Cartier
PARIS
NEW-YORK
LONDON

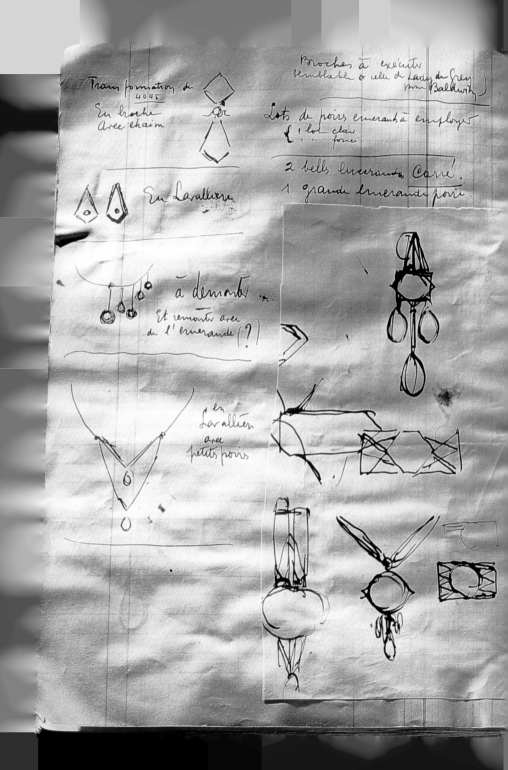

Transformation de
4045
En broche
Avec chaîne

En Lavallière

à demonter
Et remonter avec
de l'émeraude (?)

en
Lavallière
avec
petits poires

Broches à exécuter
semblable à celle de Lady du Grey
(von Baldwin)

Lots de poires émeraude à employer
{ 1 lot clair
  1 " foncé

2 belles émeraudes Carré.
1 grande émeraude poire

gd Diadème poires fond au carré
pt Diadème poires fond marquises
grand devant de corsage chaîne
médaille fleur de lys centre losange
médaille Tout en six poires et chaîne
2 petits Diadèmes 2000
Diamant bleu terminé
Perles noires à remonter
gd poire à remonter en collier
1 Lavallière 2 navettes
Lavallière 2 poires

Toupies à fleurs de
dans dans le

"	17	93		Pend d'oreille or mat	"	"	70 "
"	"	"	Fritz	et or rouge perle et			"
"	"	"		ms berles	70	"	"
"	"	94		Pend d'oreille or mat	"	"	71 "
"	"	"	"	et or rouge turquoises	"	"	"
"	"	"	"	et Perles.	65	"	"
"	"	95	"	Pend d'oreille anneaux or	"	"	70 "
"	"			rouge rubis perles	65	"	"
"	24	96	Martincourt	Pend d'oreille or poli	"	"	74 "
"	"	"		anneaux 3 perles	20	"	"
"	"	97	G. Vattan	Pend d'oreille or	"	"	18 "
"	"	"		rouge reperce et platine	"	"	don
"	"	"	"	Monture et roses 160	"	"	"
"	"	"	"	14 perles 20g. 64	224	"	"
"	"	98	Fouquet	Pend or rouge reperce	"	"	74 Fm
"	"	"		applique roses argent	"	"	"
"	"	"		Monture 205. 28 Roses 7/32 49	"	"	"
"	"	"	"	Ecrin 10.	264	"	"
"	30	99	Vattan	Pend d'oreille onyx	"	"	18 "
"	"	"		20 Perles 27 grs 5 135	"	"	x "
"	"	"		6 Roses 13/32 73 50			
"	"	"		Monture 140			
"	"	"		Ecrin 10 - 358	"		

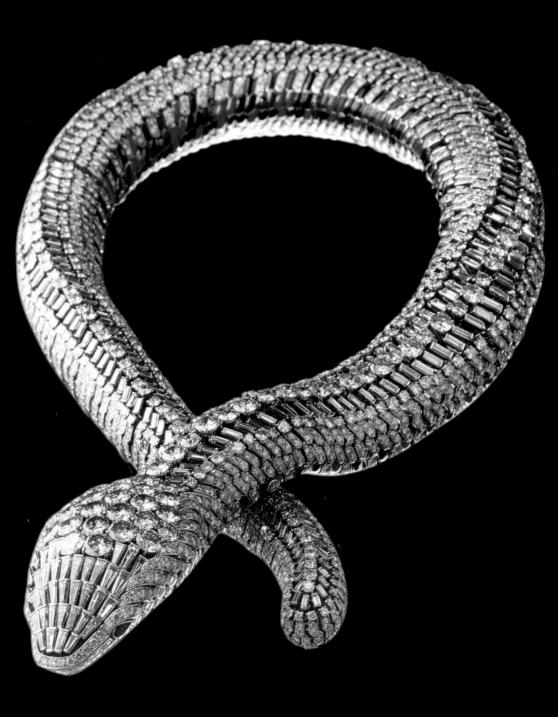

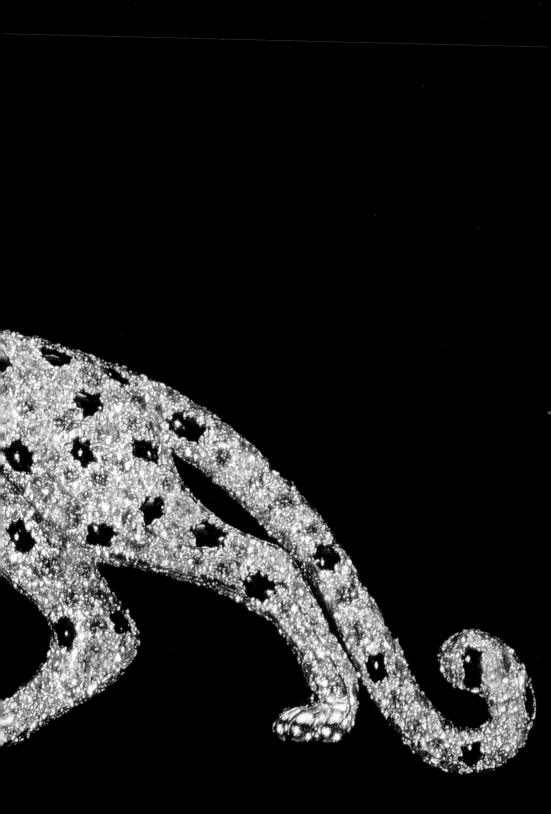

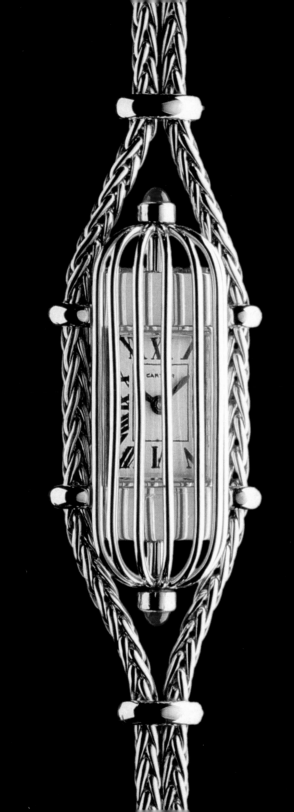

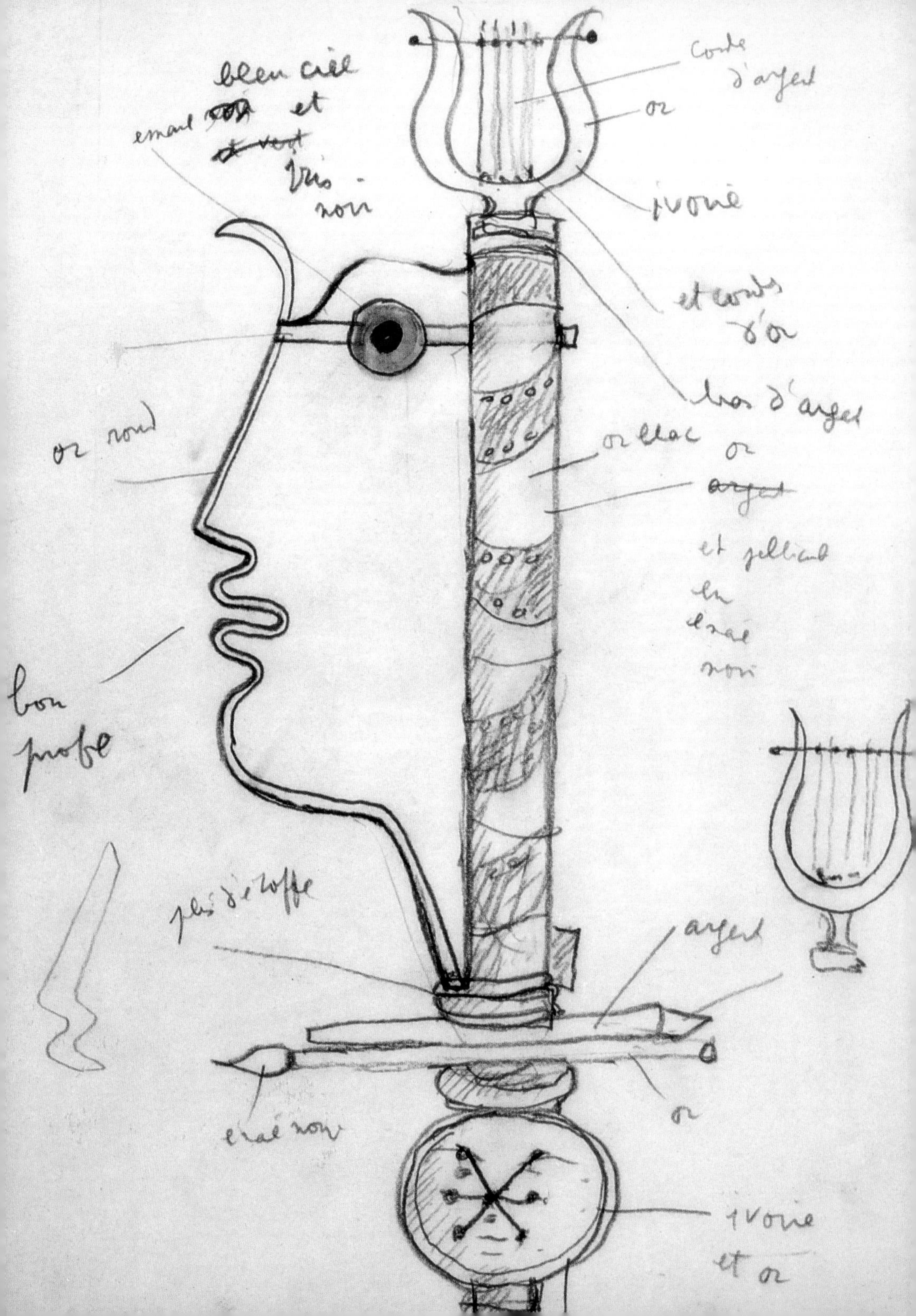

bleu ciel
email ~~vert~~ et
~~y vert~~
iris — non
non

Corde d'argent

or

ivoire

or rond

et cordes d'or

bras d'argent

or lilac ou
~~argent~~

et feuillant
en
émail
noir

bon
profil

plis d'étoffe

argent

or

émail noir

ivoire
et or

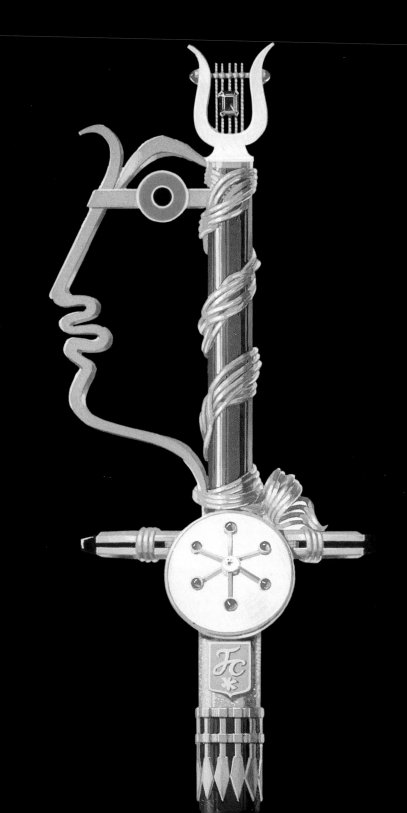

Chronology

1847   Louis-François Cartier takes over Adolphe Picard's jewelry workshop at 31 Rue Montorgueil, Paris.

1853   Cartier business moves to 5 Rue Neuve-des-Petits-Champs Paris, and sells to private clients.

1859   Cartier's moves to 9 Boulevard des Italiens; Empress Eugénie becomes a client.

1874   Alfred Cartier takes over management of the shop.

1898   Alfred makes his elder son Louis a partner: Alfred Cartier et Fils.

1899   The Cartier business moves to 13 Rue de la Paix.

1902   Opening of Cartier's London branch at 4 New Burlington Street.

1904   First royal warrant from Edward VII: Cartier's appointed official purveyor of jewelry to the King. Death of Louis-François Cartier. Louis Cartier produces his first leather-strap wrist watch for his friend the aviator Alberto Santos-Dumont.

1905   Warrant granted by King Carlos I of Portugal.

1906   Jacques Cartier takes over the running of the London shop. Louis and Pierre Cartier become partners: Cartier Frères. First Art Deco pieces in abstract, geometric form. Leather-strap wrist watch 'Tonneau'.

1907   First exhibition in St Petersburg at the Grand Hôtel d'Europe. Imperial warrant granted by Tsar Nicholas II of Russia. Contract with Edmond Jaeger.

1908   Royal warrant granted by King Paramindr Maha Chulalongkorn of Siam.

1909   New address for Cartier's London branch: 175–176 New Bond Street. Pierre Cartier opens a branch in New York at 712 Fifth Avenue. Charles Jacqueau joins the firm.

1910   Sale of 'Hope' diamond by Pierre. First appearance of locking Cs motif.

1912   Paris City Council presents Tsar Nicholas II with Cartier 'Imperial Egg' (now in the Metropolitan Museum, New York). First baguette-cut diamonds; first 'Comet' clocks.

1914   Watch bearing first Panther motif in diamonds and onyx. Warrant granted by Philippe, Duc d'Orléans.

1919   Commercial exploitation of 'Tank' watch. Foundation of European Watch and Clock Company Inc. Royal warrant granted by King Albert I of Belgium.

1921   Warrant granted by the Prince of Wales (the future King Edward VIII). Cartier Frères becomes Cartier S.A.

1924   Gold triple rings and bracelet in three colours.

1925   Death of Alfred Cartier. Jewelry exhibited in the Pavillon d'Élégance at the Exposition Internationale des Arts Décoratifs et Industriels Modernes, Paris.

1933   Jeanne Toussaint appointed director of haute joaillerie. Cartier's patents the concealed movement of 'mystery clocks'.

1938   Opening of Cartier's branch in Cannes. The smallest wrist-watch in the world, signed Cartier, presented to Princess Elizabeth of England, then aged 12.

1941   General de Gaulle founds wartime 'Free French' movement and receives crucial support from Cartier's in London.

1942   Death of Louis Cartier and of Jacques Cartier.

1945   Pierre Cartier takes control of Cartier's in Paris. Jean-Jacques (son of Jacques) takes over the London business.

1948	Claude Cartier (son of Louis) takes control of Cartier's in New York. The Duchess of Windsor orders Panther brooch.
1964	Death of Pierre Cartier.
1968	Marketing of *de luxe* oval lighter.
1969	Cartier's acquires pear-shaped diamond weighing 69.42 carats, which is sold to Richard Burton and presented to his wife Elizabeth Taylor.
1970	The 'Love' bracelet.
1972	Cartier's Paris business acquired by a group of investors assembled by Joseph Kanouï and headed by Robert Hocq. New collection of watches on sale at Cartier shops and selected concessionary outlets.
1973	Creation of boutique collection 'Les Must de Cartier' by Robert Hocq in collaboration with Alain Dominique Perrin, who is appointed managing director of this division.
1974	Launch of first collection in burgundy leather.
1976	First collection of watches in 'Must' red.
1978	Launch of Santos-Dumont watch of 1904 in gold and steel.
1979	Merger of all Cartier interests in Paris, London and New York as Cartier World. Death of Robert Hocq. Joseph Kanouï appointed President of Cartier World.
1980	Micheline Kanouï takes over the running of Création Joaillerie.
1981	Alain Dominique Perrin becomes President of Cartier S.A. and Cartier International. Launch of 'Must' and 'Santos' perfumes.
1982	First collection of Nouvelle Joaillerie: 'Le style de Cartier'.
1983	Launch of Panther watch. Foundation of Cartier archival collection. Launch of 'Must' and 'Vendôme' spectacles.
1984	Second Nouvelle Joaillerie collection: 'Les Ors et les Pierres'. Establishment of Fondation Cartier pour l'Art Contemporain.
1986	Launch of third Nouvelle Joaillerie collection: 'La Panthère'. '21' watch in steel.
1987	Launch of range of domestic items: Les Maisons de Cartier; and perfume 'Panthère'.
1988	Fourth Nouvelle Joaillerie collection: 'Egypt'.
1989	Launch of 'American Tank' watch. Exhibition 'L'Art de Cartier' at Musée du Petit Palais, Paris.
1991	Launch of fifth Nouvelle Joaillerie collection: 'La Route des Indes'.
1992	Presentation of new collection of 'Baignoire', 'Casque d'or' and 'Belle Époque' watches. Launch of 'mini-Panther' watch. Exhibition 'L'Art de Cartier' at the Hermitage Museum, St Petersburg.
1993	Launch of watches with Chronoreflex movements ('Pasha', 'Cougar' and 'Diabolo').
1994	New jewelry collection: 'Les Charmes d'or de Cartier' and three new collections of de luxe watches on the themes of 'Art Deco', 'Grande Russie' and 'Perles'. Opening of the Fondation Cartier pour l'Art Contemporain in Paris.
1995	Release of the new collection of 'Pasha' and 'Pasha C' watches. Launch of Louis Cartier fountain pen. Launch of perfume 'So Pretty'. 'L'Art de Cartier' exhibition in Japan at the Teien Museum, Tokyo.
1996	Launch of new collection of 'Tank Française' watches. Sixth Nouvelle Joaillerie exhibition: 'La Création'. Exhibition 'Cartier, Splendeurs de la Joaillerie' at Fondation de l'Hermitage, Lausanne, Switzerland.
1997	Cartier's celebrates its 150th anniversary.

Captions to illustrations

Drawings of the three historic Cartier shops: 13 Rue de la Paix (from 1899); 175–176 New Bond Street, London (from 1909); 653 Fifth Avenue, New York (from 1917). © Cartier's.
Louis Cartier on board his yacht by the shore of Lake Geneva, with his Jack Russell terrier. © Cartier's.

'Manga' bracelet-watch. Cartier's, Paris, 1991. Flexible platinum bracelet set with 498 brilliants. Photo: Didier Mansard. © Éditions Assouline.
'Marquise' ring. Cartier's, Paris, 1973. A floral ensemble consisting of 47 brilliants totalling 7.15 carats around a central marquise diamond. Platinum mount. Photo: Didier Mansard. © Éditions Assouline.

Working drawing for a ceremonial necklace made by Cartier's in Paris for the Maharajah of Patiala in 1928. It consists of five strands of 2,930 brilliants with two rubies linking the third and fourth strands. The centrepiece is the famous De Beers cushion-shaped diamond weighing 428 carats found in 1888. © Cartier's.
Photographs from Jacques Cartier's trip to Bahrain and Delhi in 1911.

The Maharajah of Patiala. © Cartier's.
'Les Éléphants', Rajasthan bracelet from the 'Route des Indes' collection. Designed in 1989, the bracelet is of yellow gold, set with 100 brilliants, 14 sapphires, 34 rubies and 28 emeralds. Photo: Tirilly. © Cartier's.

Ceremonial necklace. Cartier's, Paris, 1928, made for the Maharajah of Patiala. 586 emerald beads (total 1,218.2 carats), 4 engraved emerald plaques (63.76 carats), 565 brilliants, 496 rose-cut diamonds, silk cords and platinum mount. © Cartier's.
Ceremonial jewels made by Cartier's, Paris, 1928, for the Maharajah of Patiala. Platinum, set with diamonds; silk cords. © Cartier's.

Gouache on tracing paper of a selection of designs from 1910–20. This period marks the transition from the mannered garland style to pre-Art Deco. Archives Cartier, Paris. © Cartier's.

The premises of Cartier's, New York, at 653 Fifth Avenue, acquired from the banker Morton F. Plant in 1917 in exchange for a two-strand pearl necklace of the finest quality. © Cartier's.
Evalyn Walsh McLean wearing a necklace incorporating the famous deep-blue 'Hope' diamond, purchased from Cartier's in 1910. © UPI-Bettmann.

Pages from a 'jottings book' used by Louis Cartier, dating from 1908 or 1909. Archives Cartier, Paris. Photo: Laziz Hamani. © Éditions Assouline.

Turtle-Chimaera mystery table clock. Cartier's, Paris, 1943. Vase supported by turtle carved from coral (Chinese, nineteenth century) with brilliants. Chapter ring and base in white onyx; flower 'hand' set with brilliants indicates the hours. Photo: Louis Tirilly. © Cartier's.
'Harmonie'. A magnificent suite in platinum and gold set with rubies and diamonds, comprising necklace, bracelet, earrings and ring. From L'Album du Figaro, December 1950. Photo: Pottier. © D.R.

Necklace/tiara. Made by Cartier's, Paris, in 1947 for Barbara Hutton (Princess Troubetzkoy). The emeralds in this necklace came from the Grand Duchess Vladimir; the central emerald, weighing 100.15 carats, was formerly owned by Catherine the Great of Russia. © Cartier's.
Barbara Hutton at home in sunny Tangiers. Photo: Cecil Beaton. © Camera Press Ltd.

Eva Herzigova at the Cannes Festival, wearing the 'Adèle' necklace, made by Cartier's, Paris, in 1995, regarded as one of the finest examples of contemporary jewelry. Paris Match, 23 May 1996. © Helmut Newton.

Elizabeth Taylor photographed wearing the famous pear-shaped Burton-Taylor diamond, weighing 69.42 carats, sold by Cartier's, New York, in 1969. © Rex/Sipa Press.
The 'Adèle' necklace. It includes 291 diamonds weighing a total of 191 carats mounted in platinum. The three central pear-shaped diamonds are outstanding for their perfectly white colour (D). Photo: Didier Massard. © Éditions Assouline.

Princess Grace of Monaco seen in official portrait, wearing a Cartier necklace and tiara, 4 October 1959. Photo: G. Lukomski. © Archives du Palais Princier de Monaco.
Jane Seymour at the exhibition 'L'Art de Cartier' at the Petit Palais, Paris, 1989. She is wearing the 'Orénoque' necklace and admiring the tiara made by Cartier's in 1910 for Queen Elisabeth of Belgium. © Cartier's.

Queen Marie of Romania wearing a tiara decorated with pearls and sapphires. Cartier's received the royal warrant in 1928. © Cartier's.
The Grand Duchess Vladimir in traditional Russian costume. She wears a briolette diamond tiara inside her kokoshnik; around the base is the emerald necklace later owned by Barbara Hutton. Cartier's, Paris, 1908. © Cartier's.

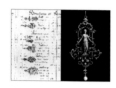

Page from Cartier's stock register. The entries run from 1893 to 1899. At this time the firm occupied premises in the Boulevard des Italiens. Archives Cartier, Paris. © Cartier's.
Pendant. Cartier's, c. 1900. Designed as a draped goddess standing on a pedestal, in gold and silver, framed by a Renaissance-style lattice set with rose-cut diamonds and brilliant-cut calibré rubies, emeralds and sapphires. Suspended from it is a large drop pearl. Photo: Louis Tirilly. © Cartier's.

The Place Vendôme, Paris, centre of the jewelry trade, a stone's throw from Cartier's premises in the Rue de la Paix. In this square Cartier's has two shops, at no. 7 and no. 23. Photo: Laziz Hamani. © Éditions Assouline.
Cartier's, London, at 175–176 New Bond Street; this has been the firm's London headquarters since 1909. Photo: J.-P. Charbonnier. Réalités anglaises, 1952. © D.R.

Design for necklace made by Cartier's, Paris, in 1947 for the Duchess of Windsor. Motifs in gold wire network set with cabochon turquoises, brilliant-cut diamonds and 29 amethysts. Pencil and gouache drawing on green tracing paper. © Cartier's.
The Duke and Duchess of Windsor dancing at a club in Palm Beach, California, March 1959. © Archive Photos.

'Paris' ring, 1946. Signet ring with hoop in fluted yellow gold; oval bezel with scalloped edge, set with two rows of brilliants around a briolette ruby mounted in gold. Photo: Louis Tirilly. © Cartier's.
'Paris' ring, 1949. Signet ring body with onyx hoop and diamonds set in yellow gold and platinum mount; oval bezel set with brilliants, with rows of baguette-cut diamonds around a central raised diamond in a setting flanked by two smaller diamonds. Photo: Louis Tirilly. © Cartier's.

Necklace. Cartier's, London, 1932. Platinum set with faceted diamonds (total weight 108.59 carats) and a rectangular emerald (143.22 carats). Photo: Louis Tirilly. © Cartier's.
'Le Flamboyant' table clock. Cartier's, Paris. Gold and silver set with 1,540 brilliants, 1 ruby, 12 emeralds, 230 green tourmalines, 230 iolites, 140 pink tourmalines, 160 citrines, mother-of-pearl, lapis lazuli and onyx. Photo: Louis Tirilly. © Cartier's.

Snake necklace. Made by Cartier's, Paris, for Maria Felix in 1968. 2,473 diamonds, some brilliant- and baguette-cut, 2 emeralds in a setting of platinum and grey gold; underside decorated overall in coloured enamel. Photo: Louis Tirilly. © Cartier's.
Bird of Paradise brooch. Cartier's, Paris, 1948. Set with 894 diamonds (total weight 92 carats). Platinum mount. Photographed for American Vogue, black velvet dress by Piguet. Photo: Kollar. © Ministry of Culture, Paris.

Jeanne Toussaint wearing the famous pearl necklace she was never without. According to Cecil Beaton, she was 'of small bird-like stature'; he was particularly struck by her 'almost male contempt for trivialities' and her sixth sense for fashion – the famous 'goût Toussaint'. Photo: Cecil Beaton. © Cartier's.
Vanity case. Commissioned 1928. Enamelled black on gold, diamond and onyx panther flanked by emerald cypresses. Photo: Louis Tirilly. © Cartier's.

'Jooghi' brooch. Cartier's, Paris, 1988. One of the most striking contemporary interpretations of a feline subject. Movement and muscle are perfectly captured in this figure encrusted with 453 brilliants interspersed with 68 sapphires. Photo: Massard. © Éditions Assouline.

Baguette bracelet watch. Cartier's, London, 1956. Yellow gold, white enamel face, Roman numerals, sword-shaped hands in blue steel. Case enclosed within a cage motif in gold wire decorated with two cabochon rubies; a double herring-bone-link chain forms the bracelet; yellow gold attachments. Photo: Louis Tirilly. © Cartier's.
Iman wearing the 'Anthiala' parure made by Cartier's, Paris, in 1991: necklace, ring, braclet in platinum and brilliants. © Vanessa von Zitzewitz.

Lucky dip at Cartier's in Paris as Madame is unable to make up her mind. Photo taken in 1950 at 13 Rue de la Paix. © Cartier's.
Square bracelet watch. Cartier's, Paris, 1912. Gold and platinum case; surround, shoulder and strap attachments bearing acanthus-leaf motifs set with brilliants; silvered face, rose-cut diamond winder, bracelet of pearls and onyx beads. Photo: Louis Tirilly. © Cartier's.

Jean Cocteau's academician's sword. Based on a design by Cocteau. In profile, Orpheus, the classical poet and musician central to Cocteau's work; handle surmounted by a lyre with an inset emerald weighing 2.84 carats given by Coco Chanel. On the ivory disc appears the six-pointed star associated with Cocteau's writings, with a cabochon ruby at each point and a central diamond given by Francine Weisweiller.

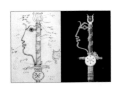

'Palm Tree' brooch. Cartier's, Paris, 1957. Platinum mount; fronds set with brilliants and baguette-cut diamonds; central cluster of seven Burmese rubies (total weight 23.10 carats); articulated trunk set with brilliants and baguette-cut diamonds. Photo: Louis Tirilly. © Cartier's.
Necklace. Cartier's, Paris. Seven square-cut emeralds and marquise diamonds suspended from a row of brilliants passed around the neck. Matching earrings. Officiel de la couture, 1951. © D.R.

'Tutti frutti' necklace. Cartier's, Paris, 1936. Platinum set with emeralds, rubies and sapphires engraved as leaves, sapphires cut, polished or engraved, with brilliants and baguette-cut diamonds; thirteen pendent briolette sapphires, two engraved sapphires on the clasp. Photo: Louis Tirilly. © Cartier.
Mrs Daisy Fellowes at the ball hosted by Carlos de Beistegui in Venice, 1951. © Robert Doisneau-Rapho.

The publishers wish to thank the house of Cartier for invaluable help in producing this book, and especially Franco Cologni, Micheline Kanouï, Éric Nussbaum, Christine Borgoltz, Corentin Quideau, Betty Jais and Michel Aliaga.

We are also indebted to Elizabeth Taylor, Jane Seymour, the Princely Family of Monaco, Helmut Newton, Eva Herzigova and Iman, as well as to Vanessa von Zitzewitz, Florine Asch, Laziz Hamani, Louis Tirilly and Didier Massard.

Finally, this book would not have been possible without the help and co-operation of various agencies. Our thanks go to: Daniela Ferro (TDR, Milan), Marie-José Eymere (L'Officiel), Catherine (Archive Photos), Cécile (Rapho), Catherine (Imapress), Martine (Rex/Sipa) and Rudi (Metropolitan).

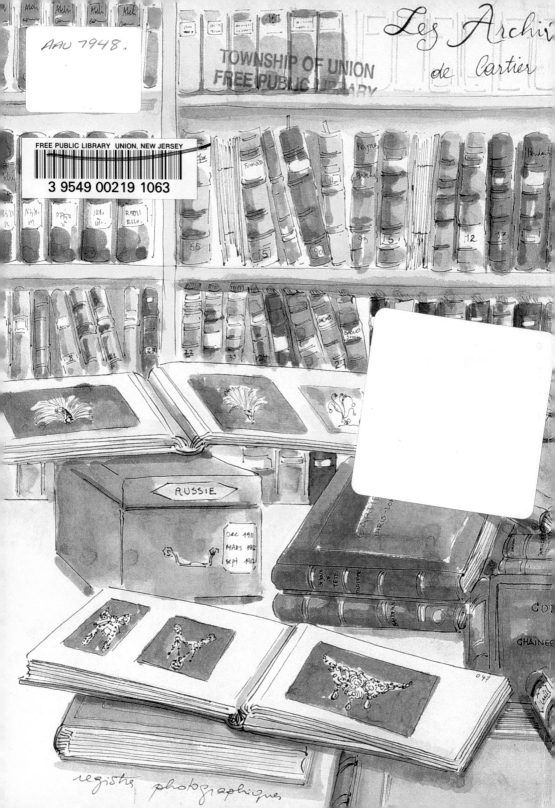

Les Archi

de Cartier

RUSSIE

DEC 1911
MARS 1912
SEPT 1912

registre photographiques